THE MIRACLES
OF GOD THAT
TOOK PLACE IN
MY LIFE

Gladys Flournoy

"Scripture references are taken from the King James Version,

New International Version and other translation of the Bible

Printed in the United States of America

First Printing, 2021

ISBN: 978-0-578-92051-1

Email: gladyslifestory@gmail.com

Table of Contents

Thankful

To the Godhead whom I love with all my heart and soul, mind and strength. My Life Story has not been without much suffering, pain, heartache, sickness disease, trauma, rejection, but I stayed persistent in prayer to God for my Deliverance.

I thank and praise God for being my healer overall. King of the universe, the creator of all things seen and unseen, He is the fruit of my life. God, you have kept me in this life You preserve me to reach this season of an open heaven, miracles, signs, wonders, and supernatural blessings in this New Year of 2021.

Dedication

I would like to dedicate this book to anyone who is believing God for a miracle of healing. If He did it for me He can do it for you.

Pray, Believe, and Trust God.

I would also like to dedicate this book to my beautiful daughters and granddaughters. You all are always in my thoughts and Prayers.

I love you all so much.

I dedicate this book to the late Apostle Ernest Leonard ministries in

New Jersey and his apostolic counselor and his prophetic team and to all my mentors who have poured into my life for over 34 years, their knowledge, wisdom, understanding, love and support. A church built upon the foundation of Prayer, Healing, and Deliverance.

Thank you all for teaching me to pray nothing but the pure word of God. Each one of you taught me how to move in the spirit of excellence. I thank God for you all correcting me when I was out of order, always encouraging me through my dark times and listening attentively to me even when I didn't have an answer. I still thank you today.

To my new mentors Apostle Travis and Pastor Stephanie Jennings and The Harvest Tabernacle Church in Lithonia Georgia.

I praise God for being under your teaching and leadership.

Thank you for everything you have done for me since I've been there.

I love you both.

Acknowledgments

First, I thank and praise God almighty for His showers of healings throughout my life. Without God, none of this would have been possible.

To my family and friends whom I love so much, You all are forever in my thoughts and Prayers. I thank God for each of you.

I would like to express my absolute gratitude to my spiritual son and daughters. I truly Thank God for you all.

Dexter & Jennifer Walker who has been such a blessing in my life.Thank you for your prayers and words of encouragement.

Denise Angrish who has been a part of my life for over 27 years what a blessing you have been in my life.

Teresa Sewell thank you for your encouragement and prayers. What a blessing you are to me.

God is a Miracle Worker

There is nothing magical about these testimonies. They are all true God brought me through every one of them. I thank God for his grace, mercy. The word of God has sustained me down through the years. I continually pray the word of God still to this day. God has already said in Psalms 138:8 The LORD will perfect that which concerneth me: thy mercy,

O,LORD, endureth for ever: forsake not the works of thine own hands.

It has always been said that No Prayer produces No Power, Little Prayer produces Little Power, Much Prayer produces Much Power. You have to determine what category you fall in. **Luke 18:1** Then Jesus told His disciples a parable to show them that they should always Pray and not give up.

God is a God of miracles. He can give you the keys to unlock the doors. Nevertheless, unless you pick them up and activate them and use them, they are useless to you.

I had gone through much suffering, pains, and sickness, trauma, emotional drain, loss of vision. It was through persistent and prevailing prayer to God for deliverance and direction into fulfilling my destiny. I pray that these testimonies can help you as you read them.

God is good, and there is nothing too hard for Him **Jeremiah 32:27**. My faith is still being tested today. I will not give up, nor give in. I have been picked and chosen by God to be his mouthpiece. I am an intercessor, a Prayer warrior that's been washed in the blood of Jesus Christ.

I decree and declare that the LORD would use me to bring forth healing and restoration to the wounded, rejected, and the brokenhearted.

In Jesus name

I decree and declare that the words that have come out of my mouth will not return to me void nor empty but they will have life and give life.

In Jesus Name

Isaiah 55:11 (KJV) So shall my word be that goeth forth out of my mouth: it shall not return unto me void, but it shall accomplish that which I please, and it shall prosper in the thing whereto I sent it.

Chapter 1

God Had His
Hands on Me

A s I look back over my life story, it was always a mystery to me. It was very complicated for me as a child. Things constantly were occurring. The devil had signaled me out as if he had a death warrant to take me out of the world. I came from a large family. My parents had nine daughters. I was the sister of eight siblings. I had to eat, sleep and get alone with them every day. We did not have very much but my mother taught us the importance of being very close. My mother was very strict and She imposed many demands and restrictions on our lives, even though I was not raised in a Christian home. As I look back over my life, God's hands were always on me. I remember at the age of 11 years old, my sister and I were playing baseball.

My sister hit the ball, However, I missed it. I ran across the street and did not look to see if anything was coming. A truck hit me and broke the tibia bone in my left leg. That was the first time that I can recall a miracle happening for me. I could have died. However, God sustained me from death. He had His hands on me at the age of 16 too. A case of pneumonia struck me until I coughed up blood and had to be put on oxygen. I almost died. That demonic spirit of death tried to take me out again.

I was diagnosed with acute respiratory problems. I have been diagnosed with pneumonia 11 more different times.

My Life Story is a book of miracles beyond miracles.

Chapter 2

Too Much to Handle

———————◆◆◆———————

In 1965 my high school sweetheart asked me to marry him. Of course, I said yes! He was the love of my life. We were so happily married in the first few years of our marriage. Over the years, things began to happen in our marriage. That we were not prepared for because of our Immaturity, unfaithfulness, disinterest, We begin to drift apart from each other not knowing how to communicate about such things.

Nevertheless, we dealt with it the best way we knew how and that was to sweep it under the rug, pretending that it was not happening. Neither one of us was saved; we did not know the LORD. So we were still drifting further apart. We started to add to our family. I had two beautiful daughters throughout our marriage. As we were trying to move forward in our marriage, my health began to challenge me.

In 1973, I had been sick off and on. It got to the point where I had to have surgery, but things didn't go well. I had many complications. I remember that my husband and my mother visited me in hospital. Although, I could not stay awake because I was having severe pains in my stomach. I would moan and groan until I fell asleep. My mom asked the doctor why I was sleeping so much? My doctor said there was nothing wrong with me. I remember my husband and mother waking me up and letting me know that they were leaving. I think I said goodbye and I fell asleep again. Sharp pains in my stomach awakened me. Those sharp pains were excruciating. I got up and made it to the restroom. I looked down at myself.

There was blood everywhere. I started yelling at the top of my lungs to get somebody to help me. I was trying to get out of the restroom to get some help from the nurse's station. When the nurses saw me, they came running in to see what had happened to me. They said to calm down. I was crying hysterically and shivering so much. The nurse said that we had just called your doctor. They called my husband and my mother too. Finally, the doctor came in and saw all the blood. He examined me and told me the place in my stomach where I had surgery came loose.

By the time my husband and mom came. They could not come in there because the nurses were cleaning up all the blood, removing the sheets, and cleaning me up as well. My husband and mom came in. They asked what had happened, doctor? The doctor replied' the surgery your wife/daughter went through caused her to be in and out of sleep also the area in her stomach that I did the surgery had come loose that is what's causing her to be in excruciating pain. He went on to say that he would not be able to take me back to surgery because the fluid from my stomach had to drain out completely and it will probably take about 10 hours.

I was so sick and scared. I thought that I would die and leave my two little beautiful girls here to grow up without me.

The next day I went back to surgery. I had an open vision. It was just like angels took me straight up to heaven and showed me how beautiful it was up there. I looked down. The doctors seemed to become angels who operated on me. I looked around, and everything was so beautiful and peaceful. I was in so much peace. When they finished operating on me, I woke up the next day with the doctor, saying they could not sew me back up. They had to put tools into my stomach to hold the drain open for about four months. The miracles of God in my life.

I am a miracle.

Chapter 3

Heartbond to Heartbreak

In 1980 my marriage was struggling. I was never taught how to be a wife nor mother. A lot of things I did not know at that time and

I still did not know Jesus. I was going to a Baptist church that did not teach about holiness, forgiveness, love, nor repentance, not knowing at that time I needed help, But I had no one to call on for help. I didn't know that I could have called on Jesus to help me.

My life turned from bad to worse. In September, I found myself running for my life. I was emotionally drained, and I felt like my body was about to collapse. I was so afraid that I would die like this. I had no word, no power, and no Jesus. In the same year of 1980, my husband and I separated. I was heartbroken. My mind was full of stuff. It became overwhelming. I was having a nervous breakdown. I ended up in a mental health hospital for about 4 months for treatments. They would give me injections and all kinds of psychotropic medications, to try to control my emotions, depression, and my mind. While being treated there somehow, they gave me a dirty needle and I contracted a virus type B hepatitis. (HBV) They later told me that it was an incurable disease caused by inflammation which causes my liver and pancreas to shut down completely. They said that I was contagious. I had to be quarantined. I was in the hospital for 97 days. I could not eat nor drink by mouth for a month. I was just laying there in the hospital bed. The doctor told my mother that she was going to lose me. They told her to prepare for the worse. All my vital signs were dropping very fast. My temp was 105, and the nurses could not bring it down. They had buckets of ice and alcohol mix washing me down. They were trying to break that fever, but nothing was working. I begin to get worse every time I would sneeze, or cough blood would drip from my nose and out of my mouth. My mother cried out with a yell. Please, God, do not take my daughter, PLEASE!...

Chapter 4

God Sent me an Angel

———— ※ ————

That night God sent an angel into my room. After 97 days of beginning in and out of consciousness in the hospital, this angel began to pray for me with the word of God. He was saying bible scriptures with me. I could hear the angel telling me to repeat **Romans 10:9-10**. "If thou will confess with their mouth the LORD Jesus and believe in their heart, that God raised Him from the dead you shall be saved. For with the heart man believe unto righteousness, and with the mouth, confession is made unto salvation."

This angel started talking about **2nd Corinthians 5-17**. In Christ Jesus, he is a new creature. The old things have passed away and beheld all things become new. I could feel the arms of that angel on me. Immediately, I sensed the strength returning to my body. Not only did I feel good, but I also felt the presence of Jesus around me. I kept repeating. I am saved, I am saved! From that moment on, I never saw that man/angel again. I knew God had sent me an angel. I started taking the word of God 3 times a day, as you would if you were taking medicine.

Proverbs 4:20-24   My child Pay attention to what I say. Listen carefully to my words. Don't lose sight of them. Let them penetrate deep into your heart, for they bring life to those who find them, and healing to their whole body. Guard your heart above all else for it determines the course of your life. I began to get stronger and stronger. I was finally discharged from the hospital, with no guarantee of life. According to the doctor, I had only three years to live with that disease. But God knows better than any of us. I am still here today and I am disease-free.

That was another miracle that the LORD had done in my life.

Chapter 5

My Walk with the Lord

---※※---

After I got out of the hospital, it did not matter what the doctor said. I was excited to be a newborn believer in Jesus Christ. I did not understand much about the spirit at that time, But I was just happy. I was on the LORD's side. I felt so peaceful and overjoyed. I told my mother I would not be returned to the Baptist church. She looked at me in awe. She could not understand why I wanted to leave the church where I grew up as a child. I told her I wanted more of Jesus. I needed more of Jesus.

I wanted to find myself a Holy Ghost-filled church teaching the word of God. One day I was in Keysville, Ga. and a Holy Ghost-filled church was there for me. I got baptized in Jesus's name. God filled me with the precious gift of the Holy Ghost. I received my prayer language. I spoke in my heavenly language {tongues} for hours. I stayed in the word of God. Daily I watched how God performed a miracle in my body and my life. I was no longer contagious and contaminated with that illness. I was totally healed in my body, and my life was getting better, but I was still struggling in my mind with low self-esteem and fear. I was so embarrassed when I met people I would think that they were laughing at me

I would think that they knew I had been in a mental institution.

My mind would tell me that people thought I was crazy. It was not clear to me at that time, but God begins to do something within my mind. I begin to think differently. The more I read the Word of God, the less I thought about what people were talking about concerning me and what they were saying. My spirit began to be renewed through the word of God. Low self-esteem had to disappear from me, and fear could not stay.

Romans 12:2 NIV

Do not conform to the pattern of this world, but be transformed by the renewing of your mind. Then you will be able to test and approve what God's will is—his good, pleasing and perfect will.

2 Timothy 1:7 KJV

For God hath not given us the spirit of fear, but of power, and of love, and a sound mind.

Months had passed. I was feeling better and better. Reading my Bible more and more. I did not stop. I kept reading. I wanted to know God and what He had called and chosen me to do in this world. Regardless of what I had been through in my body, mind, and marriage ending in a divorce.

Nevertheless, I had repented and asked God to forgive me. I

gave it all over to God. It was okay now. I just wanted Jesus and wanted what He had for me.

I remember coming home from work and laying across the bed for a brief moment. All of a sudden, I heard the spirit of God saying, I am sending you to New Jersey. So I called my sister and told her what the LORD had said to me. Her response was, you better make sure that was the voice of the LORD. She went on to say He's telling you to give up your home and job and leave your family, friends, and everything for real God said that? Now listening to my sister I question myself on did I truly hear from God? So I prayed and said these words to the LORD. LORD, If that was You speaking to me you show me a sign. That same week, the LORD revealed to me two scriptures

Isaiah 6:8 NIV Then I heard the voice of the Lord saying, "Whom shall I send? And who will go for us?"

And I said, "Here am I. Send me!"

Mark 10:28-30 NIV

Then Peter spoke up, "We have left everything to follow you!"

"Truly I tell you," Jesus replied, "no one who has left home or brothers or sisters or mother or father or children or fields for me and the gospel. Will fail to receive a hundred times as much in this present age: homes, brothers, sisters, mothers, children, and fields—along with persecutions—and in the age to come eternal life.

I told my sister what God had revealed to me. I did not doubt that He was speaking to me. I begin to prepare to move. While packing up, I begin to look over my life thus far of what I had gone through so many different sicknesses, fear, nervous breakdown, heartaches, and so much more. I was ready to embrace what God had for me in New Jersey. At the same time, I tried to grasp the fact that I was leaving my family and my friends behind, that was a lot for me to handle, but I heard God say go. So I had to obey what the spirit of God said to me. I had six rooms of furniture on a Uhaul truck and nowhere to put it. When I arrived in New Jersey, my sister and my brother-in-law and their family stayed there. They said I could move in with them until I got my place to live. I was very happy that they opened up their home to me but I still needed a place to put my furniture until I got my apartment. I received a call from Sandra Washington, a friend of mine who had just bought a house in New Jersey. She told me that I could put all my furniture in her basement until I got my apartment. It was not long after

I got my apartment and I was so excited. My sister, Prophetess Mary William who I love so much. She helped me get established in my apartment. Not only that, she taught me how to Pray in my home. What a blessing she was to me.

Now I have settled in my place. I started to feel traumatized after leaving my daughters, mom, just my entire family and friends in Georgia to a place that was unfamiliar to me. I knew I heard God tell me to go. So here I am waiting on the next instruction from the LORD. Maybe I should have asked the LORD where in New Jersey, and what am I to do when I get here, but I did not. I am here now.

Chapter 6

The New Job

In 1990 I decided to go back to school. I went to Ernest Leonard Bible School. I received 3 degrees in General, Association and Social in Christian Education. While there in Bible school I achieved so many more certificates. I am so grateful for the knowledge that was taught to me. Once I completed all my classes successfully. I want to be a help to others so I went to school again to get my Social Work certification. Which I did receive. I worked for social services in a group home with psychiatric adults and mental health conditions. It was very challenging when I first started working with the consumers. They all had behavior problems, but I began to love my job. The consumers became so attached to me. I bonded with them. I had to show them that I was one who truly cared for them.

When I look back over my life, who would have thought the very thing that tried to take over my life and put me here in a mental place is now the place where I work and I love my job. I love helping people cope with their problems in their everyday lives. I like helping them improve their lives for the better I know if God did it for me He can do it for them. I know how it is because I have been on that side where a social worker had to come and consel me.

It could have been another way in my life story, But God intervened.

Chapter 7

Miracles, Miracles, Miracles

———————✦✦———————

In 1995, I went to see the doctor who ordered my mammogram. The doctor came back and said that he had to remove the mass from my breast because the oncologist had said it was cancerous. However, my Apostle, E. Leonard laid his hands on me. He told me that God is going to heal all the tissues and cells in my body. When I came out of the recovery, the doctor came around and said I am not sure what happened but the cancer cell was gone. I was thankful and praised God for his deliverance and healing and the miracle that God performed.

In 1997 I underwent gallbladder surgery, and several gallstones were removed. Thank God for healing me.

On November 23, 2006, the day of Thanksgiving, we had a grand celebration in the church. It was a glorious day. The presence of the Lord was indeed in the place. I left the church and went to work around 5:00 P.M. I was in the kitchen helping the staff and the consumers preparing for the Thanksgiving dinners. I went to get something from the refrigerator and slipped on an area rug. That rug threw me up in the air and I felt like I was floating. When I came back down, my shoulder hit the refrigerator. I was in pain, I went to the doctor, the very next day my collarbone was broken and rotated a cuff split. I had to have two surgeries. 47% of my collarbone was removed. The rotator cuff repair of that bone was very detrimental. I do not know how something like that could have happened. But it took me out of work for six months. I did not complain. I started thanking and praising God for another healing and miracle.

It seems that each year when I went for my mammogram, it appeared that the enemy tried to show up in my breast. Since I relocated to Georgia, I had five biopsies over the course of 4 years, from 2014 -2018.

The oncologist found cancer cells again. They removed the mass and gave one round of chemo. Since then, I have been cleared every year. I was so grateful for God's hands-on me. The devil had tried many things. **Isaiah 54:17**, no weapon form against me, shall prosper every time that rises against me, shall be condemned to judge me. This is the inheritance and the righteousness of the Lord. I am a miracle.

In the year 2015 thru 2017, I experienced severe pain. The pains were unbearable. There were a lot of complications when I was walking.

The doctor recommended I go to a pain management center to receive epidural injections. Every three months, nothing was not working well. Too many needles and too much opioid medication was already too much for my body. I started having sciatic nerve pain, I began to lose my strength and had no balance. I was going from one doctor to another, they had the same answer. They told me that I needed spinal surgery. I went to see a chiropractor. I spent about a year with chiropractor Dr. Connley. He would crack my spine but It did not do any good. One day Dr. Connley said that he could not take any more money because it was not working. He said that he would recommend another doctor that he thinks could help me.

Dr. Connley referred me to a neurosurgeon Dr. Kevin Khajavi.

At Piedmont hospital, I got an appointment for a consultation. I brought all my doctor's reports and MRIs to him. As we were talking, he let me know that he was a man of God and a man of faith. We both began to speak the word of God. I felt good about this doctor. He said that God might do a miracle through him. He scheduled me to have spinal surgery on September 18, 2017. The surgery was about 4 1/2 hours long. When the surgery was over, I felt so good. I felt no more pain.

On November 6, 2017, about five weeks after the surgery, everything collapsed. The pains came back worse than before, about 5:00 A.M.

I called 911. I was screaming to the top of my voice, crying with excruciating pain. My pain had gone beyond 10. My blood pressure had elevated to 214 /117. It was continually rising because of the pain in my back and leg. The EMT took me to Emory hospital. I kept pleading with them to take me back to Piedmont hospital. The EMT said that the traffic was too congested. So they took me on to Emory where I stayed until 5:30 P.M. that day. Doctor Khajavi had me transported to Piedmont Hospital. I was admitted from November 6 through the 9th of 2017.

The nurses began to hook me up to the morphine machine. They were giving me all kinds of pain medicine. But nothing would stop the pain

Dr. Khajavi sat down and talked with my daughter. He said this was when I had to trust God. He said that he did not want to do the 3 part surgery, But it had come to that point. He had no other choice but to do it. I was interceding, crying, and praying day and night through pains and suffering. I was confessing that God is still a healer and a miracle worker in my life. **Psalms 107:20** God sent his word and healed them and delivered them from every curse and sickness of the devil.

So on November 27, 2017, I was scheduled for a 3-part surgery spinal infusion. I had to be at the hospital at 5:00 A.M.

My faith was strong. I had built myself upon the word of God and did not cry. I was not afraid because I knew my Jesus had made way for my escape. My niece was crying and she was afraid for my life. The nurse prepped and prepared me for surgery. Let my family come back to the prep room to talk to me before surgery. My pastor and her husband were there, too. They prayed for me. They rolled me into the operating room. I just began to pray in the spirit and pull the blanket over my head. The anesthesiologist came to me and said he was going to put me to sleep for the operation. They begin to start the operation. But Dr khajavi came out and talked to my family. He told them that the way this medical team was going , He said that he had to stop everything or else I wouldn't have made it. He said then he went and prayed to God. He asked God which way to go with the surgery. He said that the LORD gave him a strategy on which way he should go with this surgery. My surgery was 9 1/2 hours. I was under anesthesia just that long during my spinal surgery. I could have died from being under anesthesia so long, But God intervened.

The doctor told my family that I would not fully walk until about one year. After I was discharged from Piedmont hospital to the scepter rehabilitation for physical therapy for one month, then I had an occupational and physical therapist, a nurse, and a home health aide come out to the house for three months to continue my therapy, and he;p to make sure that my hygiene is maintained my hygiene . I was walking within three and a half months after that.

I begin to sing the song Praise Him, Praise Him Praise Him Praise Him Jesus, Blessed Savior He's worthy to be praised. Oh my soul begins to rejoice.

I was on my own but that was ok because man's extremities are God's opportunity to do miracles.

When men say no, but God said yes. I do not care what you are going through. Believe that God will heal you. He is Jehovah Rapha, the most outstanding physician who can heal you and set you free.

Who the son set free is free indeed

Daily Prayers

I have put some prayers together for you to pray daily. These are the prayers that I prayed, and still, pray them today. I am still alive.

Planted by the rivers of water, my leaf will not wither. I am full of God's grace, vigor, strength, vitality, and I have a long life. I Pray that these Prayers will help and deliver you. In Jesus name Amen

Prayer 1

For Deliverance
From Rejection

—————————※※—————————

Father, forgive me for all sins. I repent for all sins that open the door to rejection (Name them if the Holy Spirit brings them to you) I forgive everyone who ever hurt me persecuted me. I asked you, Lord, to help me so that I can forgive them now, Lord. I bless them all in Jesus' name. I also forgive myself for everything I have done in the past. Under the blood of Jesus, who washes clean for a fresh start with Jesus and never to be remembered again **Mark 7:19,** I come out of the agreement with rejection and abandonment in Jesus name. I bind the strong man and all the Deliverance blockers in Jesus' name. I burst down all demonic Walls within the earthquake of the Lord in Jesus' name.

Father, in the name of Jesus, we ask for the Holy Spirit fire. I bind and cast out sabotage and rejection. I ask father that you pull out all the roots of mistrust and rejection in Jesus's name! Come out in the name of Jesus never to return to worrying again double-mindedness. Unworthy and fear go in Jesus' name, witchcraft go in Jesus name. I cut it off right now. I lose angels to drag all these spirits out of my mind, blood, and body in Jesus' name. All astro- projection I cut you off as well as all familiar spirits in Jesus' name.

I rejected every demonic spirit of rejection that was cut off from the cross. I am accepted in the beloved by my Lord Jesus Christ. I draw My Love for You, Lord Jesus. You are my strength. The unloved spirit goes now. You are a liar. I rebuke you in the name of Jesus. Go never to return in the name of Jesus. I cast out the inherited spirit of rejection that has been passed down to me by my ancestors. I forgive my ancestors for passing

That rejected spirit down to me. I cast out all demonic forms of rejection, fear of rejection, self-rejection, perceived rejection in the name of Jesus. I cast out every spirit of rejection. I cast out the spirit of the fear of rejection. Self-rejection proceeds rejection that may have entered my life at any time.

I close every door against the spirit of rejection and cancel every legal right. Rejection has had to operate in my life. I command the spirit of inherited rejection, fear of rejection. Self-rejection perceived rejection to lose their hope in me now—the mighty name of Jesus in the name of Jesus. I address the spirit of rejection, anxiety, persecution, and loneliness in my life. I command you to leave me now. Your legal right to operate in my life has been taken away. You must go now in the name of Jesus and never come back. The spirit of rejection goes now in the name of Jesus. I forbid you to operate in my life ever again. You have no authority. I cashed you out now out of darkness, never to return. in Jesus name

Prayer 2

Breaking the Spirit
of Depression

———————❋❋———————

Heavenly Father, I know that you have a plan for my life. It is meant to prosper me and not harm me and to restore hope for my future. Today I choose to rise in that hope. Use the anointing blood of Jesus Christ as my weapon. I release the blood of Jesus Christ over every spirit of darkness and associated with the strong man of heaviness. I bind the spirit of depression that has harassed me doing this pandemic in the name of Jesus. The blood of Jesus Christ, I bring àll prayers, thoughts, and words that have been spoken over me or by me under the judgment of Christ. I declare to every spirit attached to these words that you are subject to the blood-covered judgment of Jesus Christ. I come against the spirit of depression and despair, confusion, dejection, rejection, anxiety attack, fear, the spirit of shame, the spirit of guilt, the spirit of frustration, and against anything that has taken away my peace and tranquility. In Jesus' mighty name, may I find God's peace in the passing of human understanding today? In Jesus' mighty name, I pray that the hands of the Lord lift me up and out of that pit of depression and despair every door. I open, and every demon that is responsible for my pain be destroyed now in Jesus' mighty name. I bind the pain I am carrying. Be it emotional, medical, rhetorical, financial or even marital, may the Lord restore me through his word. Every gateway that's open to the enemy of depression. I shed and seal it with the blood of Jesus.

I pray for divine intervention today in Jesus' mighty name. I pray the sun of righteousness will rise with healing on his wings over me and drop me with heavy medicines of comfort, peace, and restoration even now in Jesus' mighty name. May, the sweet presence of the Holy Spirit overshadow me right now in Jesus' mighty name. I lost love, joy, peace, and the peace of God that defiles all understanding over me right now in the name of Jesus. I make a choice today to meditate on your truth and your words. I will no longer listen to the lives of the enemy. I pray all of this in the name of Jesus Christ amen.

Prayer 3

Breaking the Powers
Over Burdens

———————❖❖———————

Father, according to your word in **Isaiah 10:27**, "It shall come to pass in that day, that his burden shall be taken away from off their shoulder. His yoke from off their neck and the yolks shall be destroyed because of the anointing. I thank you for anointing today. Fill me with your precious Holy Spirit as I go free now in the name of Jesus."

I remove all false burdens placed on me by people and myself in the name of Jesus **1st Thessalonians 2:6**. I cast out all heavy burdens placed on my life by the enemy in the name of Jesus. I lose and untie myself from restraint to detach to disjoint divorce. Separate unhitch, get free get loose escape to break away unbind unchained unfiltered set myself free release unlocked liberated disconnect me from all relationships designed to keep me under the weight of heavy burdens in the mighty name of Jesus. Lord, let your anointing break the enemy's burden off from off my neck. Let every yoke be destroyed. **Isaiah 10:27** removes my shoulder from every burden **Psalms 81:6**. I cast my cares upon the Lord **1 Peter 5:7**. I kiss my burdens upon you, Lord. You will sustain me **Psalms 55:22** Lord Jesus break the yoke of the enemy's burden and break the staff and the rod of the oppressor as in the day of median **Isaiah 9:4**. Let every yoke of poverty be destroyed in the name of Jesus. Let every yoke of sickness be destroyed in the name of Jesus. Let every yoga bondage be destroyed in the name of Jesus **Galatians 5:1**. Let every unequal yoke be broken in the name of Jesus **2nd Corinthians 6:14** and destroy every yoke and burden of religion and legalism on.

My life by religious leaders in the name of Jesus, **Matthew 23:4**. I cast out every burdensome stone to be released from my life now in the name of Jesus **Zechariah 12:3**. I take upon my life through the yoke and burden of Jesus Christ for his yoke is easy and his burdens on the light in Jesus name

Prayer 4

Reversing Generational Consequences And Curses

———— ❧❧ ————

Father, I praise you for the redemptive power in the blood of Jesus and redeeming me from the curse of the law. Now, I ask you to forgive me for all the sins that I have given the enemy the legal right to place any curse on me. My household in Jesus' name by your precious blood washes me clean from all sins in Jesus' name. I now take authority over every curse spell and enchantment upon my life and command all curses issued against me to be broken. I command all evil spirits associated with any curse to leave me now. I take authority over inherit curses and command them to be broken now in the name of Jesus

In the name of Jesus, I declare that every legal possession in every legal territory of the enemy has been disarmed and destroyed. Satan has no hold over me now through curses or occult practice through sanctifications or rituals of any kind through the blood of Jesus Christ. Now, I am free. Thank you, Jesus, for setting me free. I ordered these curses and claimed to be utterly disarmed and dismantled through the power of the blood of Jesus Christ. In His name, I take authority over curses emanating from my ancestral line and command them to be broken now. I break any curse which may be in my parent's families back to 10 generations in Jesus' name. I cast out and break all curses put on my family line and my descendants.

I come in every evil spirit of any curse and spells to release me and go now. I break Every curse of constraint failure working in my family in the name of Jesus. I take authority over every curse of stagnation in my family. I cancel the consequences and evil effects of all curses. I command all spirits of pride, stubbornness, disobedience, rebellion, self Wheels selfishness in all spirits of addiction to come out of my appetite. I command all spirits of witchcraft, sorcery, divination, and occultism to come out in the name of Jesus. I command all spirits operating in my head, eyes, mouth, tongue, and throat to come out. I command all spirits operating in my chest and lung, my back spine, my stomach, navel, abdomen. All spirits operating in my heart, spleen, kidneys, liver, and pancreas spirits are operating in my sexual organs to come out in the name of Jesus. I'm breaking and canceling every curse placed on my children to punish their parents in my life. I break and cancel Every curse placed on me out of jealousy. Father, thank you for delivering me from all curses, spells, and enchantments in Jesus' name. I now claim every spiritual blessing that my heavenly father has given to me in Christ Jesus **Ephesians 1:3**. I claim those blessings right here in the very place of all cursing by the authority and power of the Lord Jesus Christ and in his name Jesus. May these things be fully accomplished and now through your mighty name. I give you thanks and honor and praise all of this. I Pray by the authority and in the mighty name of the Lord Jesus Christ of Nazareth who came in the flesh.

Prayer 5

Deliverance from Broken Heartedness

———————— ❧ ❧ ————————

Father, your word reminds us in **Philippians 4:7**, and the peace of God has transcended. All understanding will guard your heart and your mind in Christ Jesus also in **Philemon 1:7**.Your love has given me great joy and encouragement because your brother has refreshed the hearts of theLord's people. Heavenly Father, I believe that you are the gate. Whoever enters through you will be saved. I may come in and go out and find a pasture.

Lord, your presence brings me life. I thank you for the fullness of life, Lord. when I win my heart is heavy. My flesh and my heart May fail, but God is the strength of my heart and my portion forever **Psalms 73:26**. I come before you repenting of the sin of heaviness and a broken heartedness in my life. I asked for your forgiveness Now. Jesus' pain brings healing to My broken heart. His work on the cross sets me free and heals my wounds. Father, thank you for delivering me from all heaviness of heart. You rescue me from every evil deed and are bringing me safely unto your heavenly Kingdom in Jesus' name. Your word says that the weapons of our warfare are not carnal. But there are mighty through God to the pulling down of strongholds casting down imaginations and every high thing that exalt itself against the knowledge of God and bringing into captivity every thought to The obedience of Christ **2nd Corinthians 10:4-5** .thank you, Father, for healing and deliverance me from stubborn arguments, reasoning and ideas that have been lost in my mind in Jesus' name. I lose myself from emotional stress, pain in the body, and heartaches that open the door to mental disease during the pandemic. I will not be conformed to this world, but I will be transformed by the renewing of my mind **Romans 12:2**. I break the powers of deep distress, sadness, and regret, especially for the loss of someone or something dearly loved.

Lord, I cast out the spirit of trauma and depression. I command these spirits to leave me now. I declare that I am washed and cleansed in the blood of Jesus Christ. I bind every behavior disorder that causes physical and emotional injury in the name of Jesus.

I take authority and cast out spirits of hurt, doubt, and disappointment that comes because of divorce, estrangement from family members and bitter ending a friendship. I loose myself from every disappointment and hurt that opens the door to heartbreak in Jesus' name. I command the spirits of guilt, shame, feelings of allowing annihilation and suicide to leave me now in Jesus' name. I canceled the assignment against my life. I closed the door to these spirits and established God as the new door people over my life and ministry in Jesus' name.

I cast out spirits up the isolation, melancholy heaviness, and depression. Father, You sent your Son to bind up the brokenhearted, to proclaim liberty to the captives and the opening of the prison doors to those who are bound **Isaiah 61:1**. I therefore declare. I am free, and whom the Son sets free is free indeed. I am free to live a prosperous life. Every evil spirit must leave me now in Jesus' name, amen.

Prayer 6

Breaking the
Spirit of Trauma

———————— ❦ ————————

Father, in Jesus' name, I asked that you bring peace to come and establish your Dominion of Peace in me and manifest yourself in such a way that I will know that you are here. Allow me to feel the depths of your love. I rebuke any force of darkness that seeks to harm me in any way or have tried to keep me locked in this prison of trauma. You have not given me a spirit of fear but of love, power, and soundness of mind. That is what I claim today. I commend every demon of pain, trauma, shock, fear, terror, and shame to come out, I take It all to the foot of the cross of Jesus Christ, you suffered and died for me. I thank you for all that you accomplished for me.

Pour out your loving grace on me . By the power of the holy spirit remove any traumatic memory that has been stored in the cells of my mind body and restore the cells to perfect order and vibration for a complete state of healing to come Now! I commend every demon of trauma experienced in the womb, absorbed from the womb or pass down through the generations. I command the demon of DNA to come out of stock trauma, fear, terror and Shame that has come through. My generational flow comes out now in Jesus' name. I plead the blood of Jesus Christ firmly between my soul and family generations. I command that all iniquity be stopped at the Cross of Christ. Forgive those in my generations who traumatized others or manipulate, dominate or control through fear and torment. Release your precious blood and heal all unresolved grief and pain.

I command every demon of shock, trauma , fear , terror that I experienced in my life. I cast you out of my soul-conscious memory, unconscious memory, and subconscious memory and remove all shock, trauma, fear and shame.

The pain that has caused so much torment to come out now in Jesus' name.

Heal the amygdala and remove all shock trauma, fear, terror, and shame from the emotions. I ask that you, LORD, bring healing to the fear center of my brain, turn off the anxiety that I have been present for so long and replace the fear, dread and hypervigilance with godly discernment that commands every demon of trauma from my eyes, ears wash over any images seared" upon the soul with the blood of Jesus Christ. Remove the trauma from any word spoken and remove any disharmony disease or disorder that these words or images have caused. Come Out Now , In Jesus name! Remove any trauma of shame that is associated with scent. Remove any trauma from the skin. I come against trauma that has shaken me to the very core of my foundation every demon of shock, trauma, fear, and shame from my will, spirit, and soul to come out.

Lord, I ask you to restore my will and strengthen me in every way. I command every demon of shock, trauma, fear, terror and shame from the muscles, ligaments, tendons, bones, and bone marrow come out in the name of Jesus. Lord, bring your healing power to every area where my soul, body, and spirit has been crushed or broken and restore health and healing and wholeness and Jesus name amen

Prayer 7

Prayers for Deliverance
from Bitterness

F ather the name of Jesus, I present myself before you completely humbled and submitted. I ask that you begin to expose every root of bitterness operating and hiding in my life. I pray that your Holy Spirit will arise on my behalf and begin to open my eyes to precisely uproot every form of bitterness lodged in my life.

Father, I choose to forgive(Put Names here) those who have hurt and mistreated me.

LORD, I ask that you heal my soul and completely renew my emotions. I repent to you, Father, and confess my rebellion and sins that I have committed. I asked for forgiveness for holding on to the grudges and bitterness. LORD, cleanses my heart, and my mind. Provide me the strength and Grace to fully obey you. I choose to fall out of agreement with any symptoms and past experiences that generated bitterness, by the power of the Holy Spirit. I break and renounce all ungodly soul ties from past relationships and experiences. I cast out spirits of hurt and deep hurt out of my life due to my past and present relationship, Father. I ask that you free me from any fear, torment, or intimidation from past or present relationships, Lord. I pray that angels will be released to war on my behalf. I annihilate the spirit of insecurity, resentment, and unforgiveness.

I bind up all forms of witchcraft and mind control that work to undermine my soul. I bind up the spirits of chronic contention and pride. I pray, Lord, that these spirits completely cease its operation in my life. I pray that the angels of the Lord will be activated to arrest the spirits of confusion, depression, anger, resentment, and lust for revenge. Lord, I ask that you release clarity and the ability to effectively stabilize my soul. Father with your anointing I pulled down mindsets of false love and false humility that may be working in me and Jesus' name. I renounce and cast out spirits of lust, uncleansness, fornication, adultery, homosexuality,and pornography. I am commanding these spirits to leave my life now in Jesus' name.

Father, I pray that you heal me from every spirit of rejection and replace it with the confidence of your grace. Lord forgive me for yielding to the emotional pain of bitterness and allowing it to control my life. I choose to repent and humble myself and follow your word and process for my complete deliverance. I renounce all forms of church hurt that have helped me captive from fulfilling your will and purpose in my life. Forgive me for the hurt. I have caused my leader or leaders as well as the hurtl received.

Lord, forgive me for the hurt that I caused any saints my sisters or my brothers in Christ Jesus. I forgive any saint that has caused me emotional pain. Lord help me to fully love again that I may be pleasing to you.

I cast out all spirits that came in through this coronavirus/ covid-19 to make me bitter ,sour, harsh, fierce, cruel, ruthless, relentless, and scornful. I command you to go now! give me for the sin of rebellion and anger. Forgive me for the sin I have committed in the church. Help LORD,to correct any deceptive perceptions that I have embraced. The Holy Spirit arises in my life. I submit to the process of deliverance. Cause my motives to align themselves with serenity and the spirit of integrity. Father created in me a clean heart and renew in me the right spirit. I release the love of God and his healing power over me now, LORD. I believe and release my faith in your word to restore and heal my soul completely. I speak life and prosperity to my soul. Thank you, Father, for hearing my prayer in Jesus name, amen

Prayer: 8

Breaking the
Spirit of Abuse

Father, I bring before you today all those who have been abused and have been taken advantage of my weakness. LORD forgive me for not depending on you, and opening myself up to become a victim of abuse. Lord, I forgive them and pray that you would be healed in their mind and their emotions. I pray that you would release them from all the traumatic harm and hurt. They have experienced in their past being able to handle face , knowledge and dealing with what has been done to them. I command all bloodline generational curses from my family that opened the door to abuse to be closed now. All witchcraft control dependency fears anxiety pandemic and passivity to go now! I command every spirit of abuse from my childhood from all who have taken advantage of me (name the people if you know who they are). Every demonic Spirit that has been released in my life to torment and keep me locked in an emotional prison manifests yourself now. Come out in the name of Jesus.

I break off from my mind the spirit of abuse of those who have traumatized me with demonic Powers. I cast out all ungodly satanic rituals and wickedness of abusive behavior and break any programming they have released against me in my life. That they have released against me. Uproot the harmful things that have been placed inside of me and heal the things that need to be healed. All forms of abuse personally, spiritually, naturally, physically, mentally, socially, financially come out now! I plead the blood of Jesus over my life and my family the spirit of bitterness, hatred and resentment, fear and memory recall. I cast you out in the name of Jesus. I pray **Colossians 3:21** that you hear my voice and the cries of my heart right now. Your word says that fathers must not provoke their children unless they become discouraged. I have been discouraged by the violence and abuse. I have suffered at the hands of my parents.

I pray that you would have your Divine Way in my parents' heart and my household so that the violence is no longer something that I am familiar with in Jesus' name. father. I pray **Psalms 146:7** God's righteousness, who executes Justice for the oppressed, and who gives food to the hungry. It is you Lord, for you, see the needs of your people. Lord, I thank you because you set the prisoners free. Lord, it is you who set me free despite my circumstances trying to bind me. I pray against the violence and abuse that I have suffered. I declare that your love will set me free and will keep me doing this painful time. I declare that I will not be oppressed by my parents or any abuser, because you are my God and I am victorious in you, In Jesus Name Amen.

Prayer 9

Prayer for the
Lost Vision

---※ ※---

Father God, I thank you for your Holy Spirit that gives us wisdom to know what to ask for in prayer. I come to you in the name and authority of Jesus Christ, You beloved Son. I first and foremost ask for forgiveness of sins for myself, my family, and for the sins of my ancestors. I pray that the blood of Jesus will cover the sins of our family line. Let all generational curses be broken now in their sins forgiven in Jesus' name. I know you are God of mercy, Lord Jesus you are able heal blinded eyes naturally, and spiritually. Reawakening my vision to see my purpose and the destiny you have for my life empower my spiritual discernment to remove the evil veils causing darkness in my life. Lord help me to see the type of man or woman I am ordained to be to complete the assignment predestined for me.

Romans 8:11 do not let me sin against you so that Satan will not have an advantage over me. Empower me through your Holy Spirit to obey all your commands and help me to faithfully serve you so that I will prosper throughout the days of my life in Jesus name.

Every evil veil covering the works of my hands, expired by fire in Jesus' name. I Bind and paralyzed every strong man destroying my faith in Jesus' name. Every hand of the wicked against God's plan in my life be roasted in the name of Jesus. Every evil veil in my body causing miscarriage the blood of Jesus removes it now. Satanic masking attack, hear the word of the Lord catch fire in Jesus name. By the power in the blood of Jesus I erase every Mark of disfavor in Jesus' name. Oh LORD, Let your renewing power renew my life like the eagles in the name of Jesus. God, arise and prove to my enemies that you are sovereign in my life in the name of Jesus. I attack by fire every evil observer sent to terminate my life in the name of Jesus.

Oh Lord, enough is enough let every serpent in my family depart by fire in the name of Jesus. Let every eternal cobweb spirit hiding in my body come out and roast by the fire in the name of Jesus. I claim freedom from satanic and restless dreams in the name of Jesus. Every mobile satanic veil following me to cause disappointments catch fire in Jesus' name.

Every power that does not want me to recognize my own helpers be scattered by fire in Jesus' name. I paralyzed and destroyed every evil priest hired to destroy my destiny in the name of Jesus.Every spirit of hatred upon my life. I use the blood of Jesus to wash it away in my life in Jesus' name. I refuse to wear the masks of blindness or confusion in the name of Jesus.

In whatever way man has placed an embryo of martial delay upon my life by your mercy, let it be broken and let me become fruitful to childbearing in Jesus name. Evil veils inherited from my ancestors. I cast you out in the name of Jesus. Oh Lord, appear in my destiny and remove me for your glory in the name of Jesus. Every dark cloud is covering my marriage and fruitfulness clear way by fire in the name of Jesus. Oh Lord, show forth your mighty power and disgrace powers of darkness that think they have completed their work over me in the name of Jesus. Every satanic battle on assignment causes me to lose my opportunities and divine encounters scatter in the name of Jesus. Father, in the presence of that which causes the spiritual blindness, causes my life to experience all around fruitfulness and Christ name.

Prayer 10

Breaking Free Of Guilt

F ather, you said in Romans 8:1 that there is no condemnation to those who are in Christ Jesus who do not walk according to the flesh but according to the spirit. So right now I cast out condemnation that opened the door to guilt.

Heavenly Father, you are great and greatly to be praised. I give praise to the Lord! The Lord rescues the life of the needy from the hands of the wicked. I come to you now in the name of Jesus Christ, acknowledging my sin that caused me to not live up to the expectations and standards that I have set for myself. I take responsibility and come to terms with the sins in my life. I confess my transgressions to you, oh God. I confess that I have guilt and shame in my heart. I ask you to forgive me for all my sins. Lord, I let go of the past and press towards my future. I cast out the spirits of guilt and shame that have caused me emotional pain.

I break the powers of bad relationships that have embarrassed me or have made me feel unworthy of Your love. I command the spirits of scandal and reproach to leave me now in the name of Jesus. I command these spirits to be subject to the name of Jesus and the power of His blood. Go now in Jesus' name. I cast out all the demonic spirits that have come in by this pandemic and have attached themselves, making me feel guilty for not being able to be with my loved ones who have passed away doing this pandemic and not paying my last respects. I bind you and command you to go now.

Lord, I come against spirits that cause me to be easily controlled, like a puppet on strings, or would have me to be manipulated by others. I turn from these devious waves. I command the spirits of manipulation to dry up now in Jesus' name. LORD. I will possess my body a sanctification and honor, according to your word in Jesus name'. I break the powers of having a poor self-image and low self-esteem because of bad decisions I made. I lose into my life positive self-image and self-worth. I command the spirits of self-doubt, not feeling good about myself, constantly worrying that something is wrong, unable to function in daily life, and spirits that came in my early childhood through parents to leave me now. In the name of Jesus am confident that he that has begun a good work in me will carry it to completion until the day of Jesus Christ. I repent of all grudges that I have held against anyone in Jesus' name. Lord, I break the powers of deep-seated resentment and ill will towards others. I asked you to repair every relationship that my words have torn down, my actions towards others, and my belief. Help me, oh God, to make better life choices to choose better friends and develop relationships based on godly values and not based on worldly ways in Jesus' name.

Prayer: 11

Breaking the Spirit
Of Infirmities

Lord Jesus, forgive me for the sins I have committed that have opened the doors to the spirit of infirmity. I repent of them now! LORD, I forgive those who have offended me. I bind and cast out all bitterness and resentment concerning them. I bless those that curse me. Thank you, Jesus, for hearing me and forgiving me for my unforgiveness. In Jesus' name. I bind you Satan and your demonic spirits of infirmity and death. I cast them out now in Jesus's name. I bind and cast out the illness of (name whatever the illness is) I put the blood of Jesus at the root at which they came in. I closed those doors now. I seal them with the blood of Jesus. I send them to Jesus for judgment and forbid them to come back or to touch anyone else on the way. Satan you and your demonic forces are defeated. Go now, leave in Jesus' name. I lose now upon myself health and strength instead of sickness and disease. I lose the healing power of Jesus Christ of Nazareth. I lose the Holy Spirit to the max to cleanse, purify and heal. I lose your anointing power on me, Jesus.

I command my body to come into balance. Everything that is out of balance I command you to come into balance. I commend my body to function as it should. I lose balance! Balance! I lose Jesus'

Healing power cleanses me LORD, cleanse. You sent your word and healed our diseases, so Lord, I know you said it in your word. It is written into every cell of my body. I speak healing and life into every fiber of my being. Father, I thank you that by Jesus stripes, I am healed. I shall live and not die and declare the works of the Father. I cast out all curses of infirmity from my inheritance.

(Say the last names of your family bloodline on both sides) I nailed them now to the cross of Jesus Christ and Deem them null and void . Satan, they No longer exist. I send them right back to Adam. I reverse the curse. I nullify the poison in me from these families. I cancel all words spoken against me from any of my family members. I cut all negative soul ties with them. I stand separated and apart from them. I cancel every assignment of the enemy on me of infirmity through them. I bind every demon connection to those curses. I put the blood of Jesus Christ against them. I send them to Jesus for judgment and forbid them to come back. In Jesus' name, amen.

Prayer 12

Breaking the Spirit
of Loneliness

———————————— ✺ ————————————

Father, you declare to be a Father to the fatherless, a defender of widows, God is in his holy dwelling. God sets the lonely and families he leaves out the prisoners with singing. But the rebellious live in a sun scorching land **Psalm 68: 5-6** Heavenly Father, there is nothing profitable about loneliness. Lord God, loneliness destroys the body, soul, and spirit. It is Satan's subtle way of establishing authority in my life. Nevertheless, I believe your word which says, and you shall know the truth and the truth shall set you free. Jesus I stand on your truth that you are my defender you lead me out of prison with singing loneliness has no place in me or power over me. In Jesus' name, amen.

I repent for turning my back on those who love me and are concerned about my life by allowing the enemy to deceive me. I asked for your grace and power to pull down the spiritual barricade and synthetic strongholds and let your spirit, the spirit of God, prevail in my life **James 4:6.**

I break the powers of all mental and emotional problems resulting from my being isolated, separated from loved one's friends and family during this pandemic. I command spirits of loneliness, isolation, and separation from loved ones to leave me now in the name of Jesus. I close the doors to the spiritual attack that came in through the pandemic.

I canceled the assignment of all false burdens put upon me by the adversary releasing doing covid-19. **1st Peter 5:7** you are the master burden bearer. I commend my burdens in my heart and the heaviness in my soul to go now! Holy Spirit I call upon you my helper, my comforte,. I seek and embrace your peace, joy, and strength

Philippians 4:4-7

Make me hear joy and gladness that the bones which thou has broken May rejoice.

Hide thy face from my sins and blood out all my iniquities. Creating me a clean heart, oh God, and renewing the right spirit within me. LORD, I will surround myself with the right company and network with godly people. The Lord opens doors to new relationships, restore friendships with loved ones, and open new employment opportunities. Loneliness and depression have invaded my life. Restore unto me the joy of my salvation in Jesus' name.

Lord, I forgive those who have hurt me. I forgive myself. I would not keep a record of the offense. But I choose to resolve matters quickly.

Ephesians 4:26 Lord, renew my heart and cause my thoughts to always be in the word of God. I cast down all evil habits and imagination strongholds that have caused me to isolate myself. The loneliness is more than I can bear. **Romans 12:2 Philippians 4:8 ,Ephesians 4:23:30** I cast out every stubborn and unholy tenant within me and command every demonic spirit polluting me to go now. In Jesus Name.

Nothing is to Hard for God

My Brothers and Sisters I Pray that these Prayers you have just prayed help you. God is still on the throne and Jesus is always interceding on our behalf. I am so grateful for that. **Jeremiah 29:11** The Lord says, "I know the thoughts that I think towards you." Thoughts of peace and not of evil, to give you a future and a hope. God has the master plan for our lives. No matter what we face or go through in life, He is the God of Everything. Is there anything too hard for God? The answer is NO.

www.ingramcontent.com/pod-product-compliance
Lightning Source LLC
Chambersburg PA
CBHW071429040426
42445CB00012BA/1317